Crested Geckos

FROM THE EXPERTS AT
ADVANCED VIVARIUM SYSTEMS®

By Philippe de Vosjoli

Advanced Vivarium Systems®
Irvine, California

Editor: Jarelle S. Stein
Design: Michael Vincent Capozzi
Index: Rachel Rice

I-5 PUBLISHING, LLC™

Chief Executive Officer: Mark Harris
Chief Financial Officer: Nicole Fabian
Vice President, Chief Content Officer: June Kikuchi
General Manager, I-5 Press: Christopher Reggio
Editorial Director, I-5 Press: Andrew DePrisco
Art Director, I-5 Press: Mary Ann Kahn
Digital General Manager: Melissa Kauffman
Production Director: Laurie Panaggio
Production Manager: Jessica Jaensch
Marketing Director: Lisa MacDonald

Cover photography by Philippe de Vosjoli.
All photos by Philippe de Vosjoli except where otherwise indicated.
The additional photographs in this book are courtesy of Anthony Caponetto pp. 7 (top),
8 (top), 27–28, 34 (top and middle), 36 (middle), 37 (middle), 40 (bottom), 42 (top),
70 (bottom), 71 (top); Bill Love pp. 7 (middle); David Northcott pp. 11 (bottom), 13
(middle)

LCCN: 96-183295
ISBN-10: 1-882770-80-3
ISBN-13: 978-1-882770-80-9

An Imprint of I-5 Press™
A Division of I-5 Publishing, LLC
3 Burroughs
Irvine, CA 92618

We want to hear from you. What books would you like to see in the future? Please feel
free to write us with any comments on our AVS books.

Printed in China
17 16 15 14 13   4 5 6 7 8 9 10

CONTENTS

ACKNOWLEDGMENTS

A s a former biology teacher and an author of more than 25 books on keeping reptiles, I wanted to experiment with a new format that would educate through photographs rather than extensive amounts of text. I am grateful to BowTie Press (now I-5 Press) for allowing me the opportunity to assemble this type of book and for their continuing support of my herp-related writing projects. A tip of the herper hat goes to my good friends Frank Fast, who was my research partner on several field trips to New Caledonia; and Allen Repashy and Bob Mailloux, of Sandfire Dragon Ranch, for their generous help with this endeavor. Frank, Allen, and I were also the coauthors of *Rhacodactylus: The Complete Guide*, a larger work with more than 350 photos, which reflects our common obsession with this genus of geckos. As always, special thanks are owed to "Wild Bill" Love and David Northcott for coming through with outstanding photographs, as well as to Anthony Caponetto of ACJ Reptiles for his contribution of hard-to-find shots, such as examples of ontogenetic color change in crested geckos.

CHAPTER 1

GENERAL INFORMATION

B efore the early 1990s, no one could have imagined that the crested gecko (*Rhacodactylus ciliatus*, a medium-sized gecko in the family Diplodactylidae), then a rare species known from only a few museum specimens, would become one of the most popular and readily available reptiles. Several earlier expeditions to New Caledonia to find this obscure lizard (which was first described in 1866) had proven fruitless, and there were growing rumors that the crested gecko could possibly be extinct. This all changed in 1994 when, following a tropical storm, specimens were sighted on the Isle of Pines (a small island south of Grande Terre, the main island of New Caledonia). Shortly after, field trips by Wilhelm Henkel and his colleagues, and by Frank Fast and the author yielded specimens that were brought into captivity. Surprisingly, these geckos readily bred in vivaria, allowing their offspring to subsequently be distributed to herpetoculturists. Some additional crested geckos were rumored to be smuggled by unscrupulous collectors wanting to capitalize on their "rediscovery." The great majority of crested geckos in captivity originated from the Isle of Pines. Crested geckos are also found on Kutomo, next to the Isle of Pines; in several locations on southern Grande Terre; and on the Isle of Belep, north of Grande Terre. In any case, from a relatively small number of animals collected between 1994 and 1996, captive populations of this species have been growing exponentially.

Thousands of crested geckos are now captive-produced annually in the United States to meet the growing demand for this species. Besides being easy to breed, crested geckos have also turned out to be ideal pets. They are relatively small animals that have all of the features that make reptiles such fascinating creatures, including complex scalation and an unusual appearance that makes them seem like they crawled out of a fantasy story. Crested geckos are easy to house, have lower temperature requirements than many other reptiles, and for the most part are naturally tame and harmless. When kept in attractive planted vivaria, they make outstanding display animals. People who work all week and like to take weekend vacations can safely leave crested geckos for two to three days without having to resort to a pet-sitter. Based on records of animals currently in captivity, it appears that the potential longevity of crested geckos is at least 12 years, possibly much longer.

From a specialist standpoint, probably the most interesting feature of crested geckos is that they are polychromatic, naturally producing a wide range of colors and patterns. Combined with a short generation time, this has allowed hobbyists to selectively breed bright red, orange, and yellow morphs that now rank among the most beautiful of all reptiles. As attractive as these morphs may be, we have seen only the tip of the iceberg in terms of the potential this species offers for creating living works of art. In the reptile hobby, the crested gecko is destined to achieve great popularity and become the analog of the koi carp. The establishment of crested geckos in captivity ranks as one of the great accomplishments of herpetoculture.

Crested geckos reach a snout-to-vent length (SVL), the body length excluding the tail, of 4-4.7 inches (10-11.9 cm) and a total length of about 8 inches (20 cm). Adults typically weigh between 1.2 and 2.1 ounces (35 and 60 grams).

The crested gecko is found only in a primary forest, which is a type of old forest unlogged and undisturbed by human activities. The dense canopy makes it such that there is relatively little vegetation at ground level. The floor of the forest is covered with a layer of leaf litter.

The most obvious distinguishing features of crested geckos are the lateral crests that line the eyes, run along the sides of the back of the head and neck, and run partway down the back.

The crests are variable both in size and the degree to which they extend down the back. This specimen shows average-sized crests.

The width of the head and the length of the snout show a range of variation in this species. The snout is relatively long in this individual.

This individual has a broad head and relatively short snout.

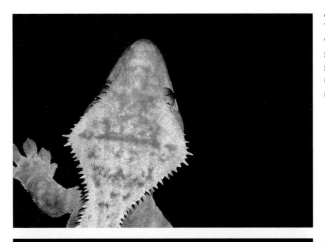

This is an overhead view of the long-snouted individual shown previously. Compare it with the next picture.

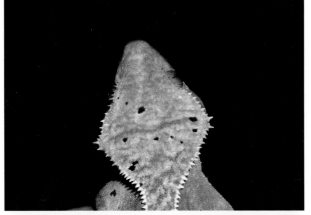

In this overhead view, the relatively short snout and wide head of this individual are obvious. The broad head trait with well-developed crests is desirable in crested geckos.

This individual shows a long snout and poorly developed crests.

Crested geckos have well-developed toe pads combined with fine claws.

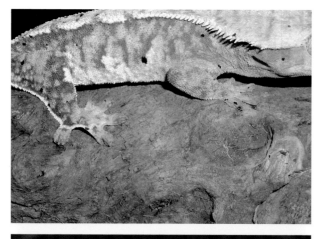

The undersides of the toes are lined with lamellae, pads of ultrafine setae that allow the gecko to cling to rough surfaces and climb on smooth ones such as glass.

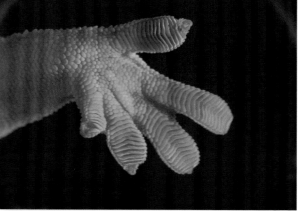

A crested gecko has a relatively long, prehensile tail. The tail tip is slightly flattened and paddle shaped.

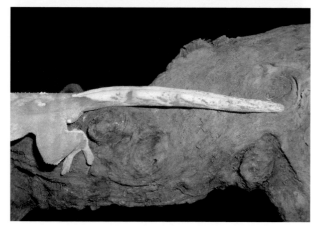

All members of the genus *Rhacodactylus* have prehensile tails capable of wrapping around tree branches or, in this case, fingers.

The underside of the tail tip also has lamellae.

Crested geckos are good jumpers. Extending the hind legs combined with straightening the body propels the gecko outward.

In the wild, the great majority of adult crested geckos are tailless. This may be the normal condition for adults of this species. Both encounters with predators and intra-species interactions may lead to tail loss.

Like all geckos, except for members of the family Eublepharidae, crested geckos lack eyelids.

When crested geckos sleep, their eyes sink into their orbits, and the upper eye rims fold down and partially cover the upper portions of the eyes.

Because they lack eyelids, crested geckos lick the lenses of their eyes to clean them.

Crested geckos are relatively nonaggressive, but if startled when sleeping under a shelter they will rise up on their legs and perform an open-mouthed threat display.

Some behaviors can be observed only in naturalistic vivaria. On several occasions I've noticed a rigid tail posture in which an animal maintains the tail extended for several minutes. This is but one indication of how much of the behavioral repertoire of crested geckos still needs to be studied.

Selecting a Crested Gecko

Begin by selecting crested geckos that appear in the prime of health. Do not waste your time by falling into the mind trap of "saving the poor skinny animals" in a store. You will be setting yourself up for heartbreak and for a waste of time and money. If you own other reptiles, introducing a sickly animal to your collection will put them all at risk of contracting a disease. The excess amount of time catering to the needs of a sick animal will take away from time spent on healthy ones.

1. Handle a specimen you are interested in. A healthy crested gecko shows activity when handled. In general, an animal that displays some activity is preferable to one that tends to just calmly lie in the hand. In lizards, passivity that is sometimes misinterpreted as docility can be a sign of illness. Go with the specimens that demonstrate some spunk.

2. Observe and feel the bones. In a healthy crested gecko, the body contours are rounded with no clear evidence of the outline of the underlying skeleton. In short, the outlines of the ribs, backbone (vertebrae), and hipbones should not be prominent. Lack of a tail or signs of a slight bend in the pelvic bones are not indicators of ill health. Being tailless appears to be the normal condition of adult crested geckos in the wild.

3. Examine the head. The eyes should appear clear with no opacities. They should be of equal size. They should not appear peculiarly large and bulged out or recessed and small. The jaw should close evenly. Avoid animals with over- or underbites.

4. Examine the toes to make sure none is missing. One or two toes missing will not affect the health of a crested gecko, but more than two toes missing on a foot can impair climbing ability.

5. As a precaution, look at the vent of a crested gecko. Most crested geckos sold in the trade are healthy and have a flush, clean anal area. Do not buy a crested gecko with smeared feces caked around the vent or with a crusty, protruding vent. These are signs of a parasitic infection or gastrointestinal disease, and you should always avoid such geckos.

6. Decide what sex you want. In captivity, the male to female ratio of captive-produced crested geckos is close to 50-50. Because breeders

aim to keep cresteds in a ratio of 1 male to 5 females, most animals currently offered in the general pet trade are "extra" males. This situation will likely change as this species becomes more common. As a pet, a male crested gecko is generally a good choice, without some of the problems that can sometimes occur after a female becomes sexually mature.

7. Decide how many you want. You can keep single crested geckos as pets. My personal observation is that, given the opportunity, crested geckos turn out to be a relatively social species. When placed in large enclosures, most prefer to spend time in close proximity to each other. I have found this to be true even when males are kept together. However, crested geckos are best segregated by size, particularly when juvenile and sub-adult. Large ones will compete with smaller ones and when hungry large ones may grab and eat tails. If the size discrepancy is too great, large individuals may even consume smaller ones.

8. Decide on your sex ratio. When they become mature, male crested geckos kept together tend to fight and compete when in the presence of females. As a rule, adult crested geckos are best kept in pairs or groups of 1 male with up to 5 females.

Handling

Crested geckos vary individually as to how calm they will be when handled. Some will linger on a hand or calmly walk up an arm, others will try to jump off at the first occasion. Picking up larger animals and letting them move about freely on a hand or arm will give you a sense of how they will respond to handling. Do not hold a crested gecko firmly, but instead use a loose, partially open grip with the hand forming a tunnel. Allow the gecko to move from hand to hand rather than grabbing it.

When picked up, crested geckos and other *Rhacodactylus* species often have a flight reaction that can be somewhat calmed by letting the animal expend energy though a procedure called hand-walking. Place a hand in front of and slightly above eye level of a loosely held crested gecko and let it climb up, repeating the process with the other hand. A restless gecko will be able to walk or hop from hand to hand.

To see how a larger gecko will respond to handling, pick it up and let it move about freely on your hand or arm.

Hold a crested gecko in a loose, partially open grip with the hand forming a tunnel.

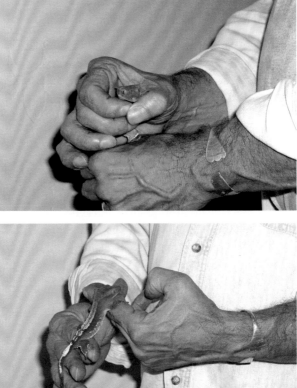

Hand-walking allows a restless gecko to walk or hop from hand to hand.

Quarantine

Quarantining is not a requirement if you are just buying one or two crested geckos that you aren't adding to a collection, but you should always quarantine newly purchased lizards you plan to introduce to a colony of established, healthy animals. Although crested geckos are usually a tough and healthy lot, pathogens from other species can infect them. Because commercial breeders often work with other kinds of lizards, and because pet stores often place animals in tanks that previously held other species, there is always the possibility that a new crested gecko could be diseased. Quarantining the new lizard allows you to monitor its health prior to introduction to an established colony. A quarantine tank should be a basic setup, not a naturalistic one. During the 30- to 60-day quarantine period, the geckos should be monitored to make sure they do not lose weight, that they are feeding regularly, and that their stools are of a normal color and consistency for the species. If you are a large-scale breeder, you may want to consider the expense of a fecal exam by a reptile veterinarian to check for parasites during this time.

CHAPTER 2

LIFE CYCLE AND SEXING

Ontogeny is the process of undergoing morphological, physiological, and behavioral changes in the course of development from embryo to adult. From a hobbyist standpoint, crested geckos undergo five broad ontogenetic stages determined by changes in morphology, growth rate, and reproductive rate: embryonic, juvenile, sexual onset, sexual maturity, and sexual decline/old age.

- *Stage 1*: The embryonic stage is spent within the confines of the egg. A number of factors affect the welfare and development of embryos, including genetics, the health and nutrient reserves of the mother, quality and moisture of the incubating medium or environment, and incubation temperature. These are all factors addressed by professional breeders as part of producing large, healthy babies of this species. This stage usually lasts from 60 to 90 days. At cool incubation temperatures in the upper 60s to low 70s F (roughly 20–23°C), it may extend to more than 120 days.

- *Stage 2*: The juvenile stage begins at hatching and is characterized by rapid growth. High-quality, frequent feeding regimes combined with optimal temperatures in the 78–82°F (25.5–28°C) range result in rapid growth. Raising animals singly can also help optimize growth because it eliminates intraspecies competition. When crested geckos are raised in groups, the more vigorous and faster-growing individuals may intimidate and in some cases eat the tails of slower-growing ones. Providing shelters that allow for segregation, such as stacked egg cartons, and regularly feeding them small crickets can greatly reduce intraspecies aggression in groups. In addition, a group should be regularly inspected for size differences and the smaller ones removed and raised in a separate enclosure. The juvenile stage usually lasts nine months to a year depending on rearing conditions. Some males reared under intensive conditions will show hemipenal bulges by as early as five months. Stage 2 ends with the ability to breed.

- *Stage 3*: At a weight around 21 grams (0.7 ounces), when crested geckos are about 3 inches (7.5 cm) SVL, you will notice in males the first signs of sexual onset. In a matter of just a few weeks, they will develop bulbous hemipenal areas behind the vent. These bulges, unlike what some may initially believe, are caused not by testes but by an enlargement of the paired hemipenes, which are everted from the tail base area in the course of mating. In females, no obvious signs of sexual onset are visible; it appears that this stage may occur a little later in females than it does in males. An effect of Stage 3 is that relative growth compared to Stage 2 continues but at a much slower rate. This is due to hormonal changes and also because energy resources are diverted toward reproduction, to some degree in males because of activity related to sex but to a larger degree due to egg production by females. This stage usually lasts one to two years.

- *Stage 4*: Sexual maturity is characterized by a stabilization of growth by about two years of age. Little size increase occurs beyond this point. This is a stage with a more or less consistent reproductive rate and can last 10 or more years.

- *Stage 5*: In the sexual decline or old age stage, egg production by females is either very low or altogether absent. In males, old age is more difficult to assess because they can remain reproductive for most of their lives. I have no good information on how long this stage can last in crested geckos. Some of the adults collected in 1995 are still alive and breeding at the time of writing (2004). A female I collected in 1994 stopped producing eggs for the last three years of her life. In leopard geckos, Stage 5 can last at least eight years. In older crested geckos, examination with a loupe often shows thickening or wear of scales depending on the area of the body. Older cresteds also have a greater tendency for shed problems, possibly because of scale thickening. The head gradually appears thinner and bonier. Eventually the lizards die from illness or old age, conditions that are usually accompanied by a gradual loss of weight. This stage ends with death.

The embryonic stage takes place in the egg.

The juvenile stage begins with hatching and lasts nine months to a year.

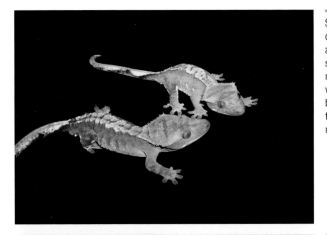

Sudden hemipenal development occurs at sexual onset. The slightly younger male on top has no visible hemipenal bulges compared to the slightly older male on the bottom.

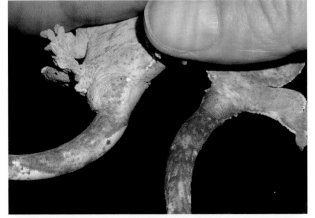

Here you see the underside of the previously pictured males, clearly showing the difference in hemipenal development during Stage 3.

The weight of animals can increase between 50 and 100 percent from the beginning of sexual onset (smaller animal pictured) to the beginning of sexual maturity (larger animal).

As a general rule, crested geckos cannot be accurately sexed until sexual onset at around 2³/₄ inches (7 cm) SVL. Juveniles will display secondary sexual characteristics when they reach that size. Guessing the sex of juveniles is based on a very slight, barely noticeable difference in the size of the postanal tail base and of the cloacal spurs, but this is not very reliable.

The earliest secondary sexual characteristic that distinguishes males from females is the development of preanal pore dots in males. These can only be observed with an 8x or higher magnification loupe. Pore development is presumed to be triggered by an increase in testosterone so it coincides with the beginning of hemipenal enlargement. However, the first signs of pores will precede hemipenal development that can be detected visually by at least a month. After sexual onset, the difference between males and females becomes obvious because males display prominent hemipenal bulges. In comparison to males, females have a relatively flat postanal tail base. Both sexes have cloacal spurs (enlarged white scales to the sides of the vent), and males usually, but not always, have larger spurs than females. As a rule, cloacal spur size is not a reliable indicator of sex.

Vent of a juvenile crested gecko.

Preanal pores on a young male crested gecko.

One of the most useful tools for sexing geckos is a photographer's loupe. At least an 8x loupe is preferred, although individuals with good eyesight can manage with a 4x loupe. These can be purchased through photography supply stores.

Good light is required to effectively view pores with a loupe.

By sexual onset, males display prominent hemipenal bulges, and the preanal pores are well developed and observable with a standard magnifying glass.

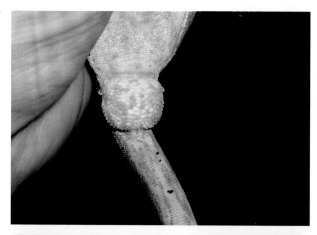

This close-up of a male's vent shows the preanal area. Note the preanal scales with well-defined central pores.

Note the female's relatively flat postanal tail base.

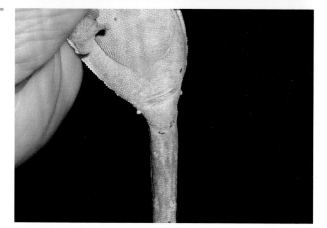

CHAPTER 3

COLOR CHANGE

Crested geckos change color with age, the shed cycle, and in response to environmental conditions. The general pattern and color of crested geckos may become darker or lighter and the reds, yellows, and oranges may become faint or bright depending on temperature and light exposure. As a rule, crested geckos usually display their brightest coloration at night and at warmer temperatures, in the upper 70s to low 80s°F (about 25 to 29°C). Most of the bright-colored crested geckos shown in photographs were shot at night.

Like all reptiles, when crested geckos enter the shed cycle their color becomes duller as the old skin detaches itself from the replacement epithelial layer. The shed skin is semitransparent, and crested geckos photographed at this stage of the shed cycle may appear bluish as a result of light diffraction.

Can One Predict the Color of Adults by Examining Juveniles?

The general pattern type of crested geckos is evident in juveniles but not the bright yellows, oranges, or reds that only develop with age. This means that patternless, dalmatian, fire, and striped crested geckos can be recognized soon after hatching, but the adult color will at best be only hinted at. Babies that can start off looking dull sometimes end up being spectacular animals. That's one reason many breeders wait until baby cresteds are five to six months old before selling them. Not only will they be able to determine sex at that age, but they will also be able to select outstanding specimens that will fetch higher prices. Interestingly, some juveniles that start off bright red may actually become rather plain by the time they mature.

A crested gecko in shed may appear duller and bluish.

This crested gecko was photographed during the day.

The previous animal photographed at night.

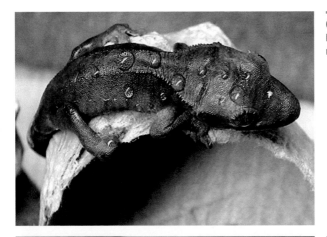

Crested gecko hatchling showing red.

By four months, the red of the previous gecko has mostly faded.

A crested gecko at three months.

The previous crested gecko at seven months.

Sibling cresteds at two months.

The previous sibling cresteds at seven months.

CHAPTER 4

MORPHS

Crested geckos are considered a polychromatic species, meaning they come in many colors and patterns. In fact, they are probably the most polychromatic of all the lizards. A probable purpose for this polychromatism is simply to effectively blend in with foliage when resting during the day. At night, bright white markings may serve as visual cues that allow crested geckos to spot other members of their species. Night is when the red and yellow coloration is the brightest. Whether this provides a survival benefit to crested geckos warrants further study. In any case, hobbyists have grouped the color and pattern types into several categories in an attempt to understand the relation of genetics to phenotype (external appearance).

- *Patternless*: Patternless crested have more or less a uniform color or faint patterning. Subcategories include brown, red, orange, yellow, tan, and olive green.
- *Brindle*: A brindle crested gecko is characterized by a light-colored background with a darker marbled pattern. Brindles are described by stating the light background color first and the dark pattern color second, such as tan and brown brindle.
- *Fire*: This morph has a light dorsal color (with some dark markings) that is separated from the rest of the body by the lateral crests. The limbs and the body color framing the light middorsal zone are of a more or less uniform darker color.
- *Harlequin*: This is a fire morph with a mottled body and limb color.
- *Dalmatian*: This crested gecko morph is speckled with varying numbers of small, usually black, spots. This is

an independent trait that can appear with any of the other color and pattern morphs. Recently, dalmatian cresteds with yellowish or orange spots have been produced.

- *Pinstriped:* Pinstriped crested geckos are fire or harlequin types with thin white lines running the length of the body crests and forming a V over the pelvic area. In pinstripe crested geckos, the lateral crests are supported by fleshy skin ridges that frame the middorsal area. Partial pinstriped crested geckos have broken white stripes
.• *Striped:* Striped is a variation of the pinstriped morph characterized by thickened fleshy ridges underlying the lateral body crests and framing the midbody area. In addition, the body patterns generally become linear (for example, spots on the sides of the body are elongated). Unlike pinstriped crested geckos, the crests are not necessarily lined with white.
- *White-fringed:* This is another independent trait characterized by a white fringe lining the thigh. In extreme forms, the postanal tail base and shins may also be lined in white.
- *White-spot:* This trait may be linked to the white-fringed trait. It is characterized by rows of white spots along the sides of the body. These often fade with age, but some individuals retain sizable white spots.

Note: Several traits can be combined, and the wildest looking crested are the result of breeding parents with different traits. For example, you can have a pinstriped, white-fringed, dalmatian, harlequin crested gecko. Obviously, abbreviated terms can be used to label these geckos such as *pwdh*.

Crested geckos naturally display a range of colors and patterns.

Buckskin crested gecko.

Chocolate crested gecko showing some pattern.

31

Red crested gecko.

Orange crested gecko.

The gold crested gecko is a new bicolored form that breeds true.

Dalmatian yellow crested gecko. The dalmatian trait (black spots) can be introduced in combination with all other morphs.

The dalmatian trait can also produce spots with coloration other than black as in the dalmatian gray crested gecko.

This orange crested gecko has broken white crests.

Red bicolor crested gecko.

A dalmatian red crested gecko showing red spots.

Orange and rust brindle crested gecko.

This is a beaded crested gecko characterized by fewer, but more enlarged, body scales.

The beaded trait is apparent in juveniles.

Crested geckos with wide heads bordered by well-developed crests supported by skin folds are called crowned.

Chevron crested geckos are characterized by rows of light blotches running down the back, resembling the chevrons on military uniforms.

Dark green fire crested gecko.

Olive fire crested gecko.

Mocha and cream fire crested gecko.

Red and orange fire crested gecko.

This fire crested gecko has some harlequin features, such as the patterned limbs.

Some morphological traits, such as unusually large eyes on this big-eyed baby crested gecko, may best be considered defects and bred out of captive colonies.

This classic example of a harlequin crested gecko shows the highly patterned body and limbs.

Partial striped harlequin crested gecko.

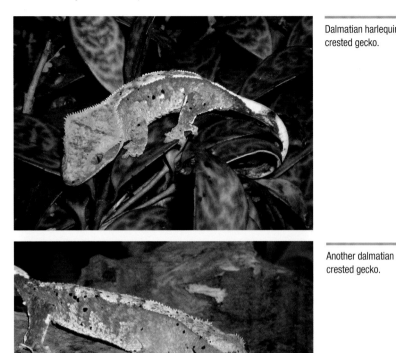

Dalmatian harlequin crested gecko.

Another dalmatian crested gecko.

This crowned harlequin crested gecko shows well-developed head crests.

A partial-striped harlequin crested gecko.

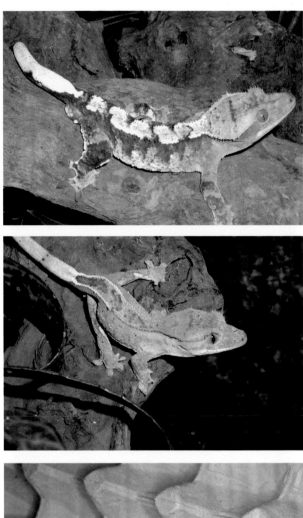

Here is an outstanding striped crested gecko.

This juvenile harlequin crested gecko has purplish coloration.

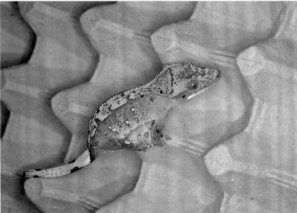

In this striped individual, the tendency for the body pattern to become elongated is clearly apparent.

Striped harlequin crested gecko.

The white-spotted trait is characterized by a row of sizable white spots along the sides.

Orange dalmatian striped crested gecko.

This striped crested gecko has an unusual pattern.

The white-shin trait is linked to the white-fringe trait.

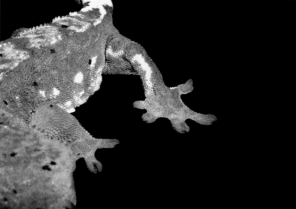

CHAPTER 5

HOUSING CRESTED GECKOS

Selecting an Enclosure

Crested gecko owners have several enclosure options depending on their goals and their environmental constraints. If your primary goal is keeping crested geckos for the purpose of enjoyment and observation of their behavior, then large glass- or plastic-sided tanks with sliding screen tops or with sliding glass fronts are the best choice. These enclosures give the impression of quality and offer good visibility for the purpose of display. In dry climates or in air-conditioned rooms, they can also help retain humidity because their solid sides will help contain moisture and reduce the rate of evaporation.

There are a few disadvantages to enclosures with sliding tops, though. They require space behind or in front of the tank to slide the top, and light fixtures may have to be removed prior to opening. Front-opening enclosures are generally more expensive than top-opening enclosures, but the many benefits, including being able to readily access all inside areas, make them well worth the extra cost. This is particularly true with large enclosures and those with a number of light fixtures on top. The main drawback with all-glass tanks is their weight.

For the purpose of maintaining large colonies for breeding, many hobbyists prefer screen-sided enclosures because they are light, stackable, and easy to clean using a spray nozzle at the end of a hose. The screened sides also provide climbing surfaces enjoyed by these lizards. A disadvantage of these cages is that they offer poor viewing and do not help raise humidity in dry climates. A good general rule is that the minimum size enclosure for housing one to three adult cresteds should be 20 gallons (76 liters), standard tank size of 24 inches long x 12 inches wide x 16 inches high (61 x 30 x 40 cm), with a 29-gallon (110-liter) tank being an even better choice. For display purposes, larger enclosures will allow you to create a more interesting and complex landscape design. These cages are typically sold for housing chameleons.

Stacked screen-sided enclosures are commonly used by breeders to house large numbers of crested geckos. The primary concern of commercial breeders is to devise systems that allow for keeping and breeding the maximum number of animals humanely in a minimum amount of space with a minimum amount of labor and at a minimum cost. To succeed as a commercial breeder of inexpensive species is a numbers game. How many animals can one produce per square foot of space and per kilowatt hour of electricity? Many people who keep crested geckos as pets opt for the lab animal system used by commercial breeders and in most pet store displays. These will keep animals alive and breeding, but you will miss out on most of the enjoyment of observing crested gecko behavior. To fully appreciate crested geckos and their range of behaviors, naturalistic vivaria are the only way to go.

Some commercial breeders, based on a system used with leopard geckos, use large, tall plastic storage containers on racks to maintain large colonies of crested geckos. When using storage containers, you should perforate the sides with one or two rows of holes using a drill or a small soldering iron to allow for ventilation and reduce the buildup of molds. If using a soldering iron, do this outdoors to reduce the risk of inhaling plastic fumes. My main complaint about plastic storage bins is that the poor visibility does not allow for good monitoring of the animals. Minimum size should be 24 inches long and 10 inches high (61 x 25 cm).

Plastic terraria come in a range of sizes, and they are ideal for quarantining new crested geckos and for housing babies. Ideally, any newly purchased crested gecko should be set up in a quarantine tank and monitored for health for at least 60 days.

By far the most widely sold enclosures for reptiles are all-glass tanks with sliding screen tops. These are relatively economical and offer good viewing from all sides. The screen top offers a good level of ventilation.

In some areas, glass tanks with both a sliding screen top and side panel can be special ordered. These tanks provide easy access and ease of maintenance. They can be placed on shelves and allow for efficient use of space.

Front opening screen-sided cages are great for keeping large colonies. The cage represented here, with a plastic bottom and two plastic sides, allows for stacking of cages.

Stacked screen-sided enclosures are commonly used by breeders to house large numbers of crested geckos.

The minimum size of large plastic storage containers should be 24 inches long and 10 inches high (61 x 25 cm).

For easy access to the inside of a naturalistic display that allows for cleaning and maintenance, sliding or hinged glass of Plexiglas-fronted enclosures are the best.

Basic Setups

Crested geckos are easily maintained in simple setups with either newsprint or artificial carpet as a substrate. The minimum landscaping should consist of potted plants, such as *Ficus benjamina* or *pothos*, or wood branches or wire frames with live or artificial foliage running through them. In addition, a ground shelter, such as a piece of curled cork bark, should be placed on the floor. Add a shallow container to provide water. Crested geckos will fare well and breed in these bare-bones setups even without additional light or heat as long as they are kept at comfortably warm room temperatures in the mid- to upper 70s F (24–26°C). Adding a low-wattage incandescent bulb on top of screen-covered enclosures provides additional heat as well as light for viewing and for growing plants. Simple setups are recommended when quarantining animals. For the purpose of enjoyment, planted naturalistic vivaria will be much more rewarding, both as decoration and for the opportunity to observe a greater range of behaviors.

Specialist Allen Repashy has experimented with many options for optimizing commercial breeding of *Rhacodactylus* species. After initially trying artificial plants on wire frames, he shifted to using vertically stacked large egg cartons. This system greatly increases the internal surface area of the setup and provides multiple shelters and activity areas that segregate the animals both visually and physically. By reducing the amount of wall space in the enclosure, egg cartons can also reduce the propensity for crested geckos to rest vertically on the walls, a behavior that contributes to the incidence of floppy-tail.

Substrates

An advantage of using soils as substrates is that they can become bioactive and break down waste matter. You first need to use a potting soil that includes some coarse organic matter, such as peat moss and ground bark, but does not contain perlite. The perlite tends to float to the surface, is unsightly, and is sometimes eaten by lizards. Mixing in a drainage component to make the soil looser and increase airiness generally is beneficial. Adding 10–15 percent by volume of seedling orchid bark, coarse sand, fired clays (such as the pellets used for growing plants hydroponically), or fired diatomaceous earth pellets (for example, Isolite) helps aerate the soil and prevent it from compacting.

Before adding the soil to your vivarium, place at least a 1-inch (2.5-cm) drainage layer of gravel or hydroponic clay pellets at the bottom of the vivarium before adding a soil-type substrate. A lightweight alternative is to place a layer of egg-crate plastic (sold as fluorescent light shields in hardware stores) covered with plastic screening.

Place at least a 1.5-inch-thick (3.8 cm) layer of soil on the bottom and add water so it feels just moist, but not soggy. You can then introduce plants and landscape to the vivarium. The trick to bioactivating a substrate is to: 1) weekly spray the inside of the tank and soil surface; and 2) weekly stir the surface of the soil layer down to half its depth with a utensil such as a large plastic serving fork. Spraying allows waste matter to fall to the surface and keeps the soil moist. Stirring moves waste matter (feces and urates) to the moist section of soil where it can be broken down by bacteria. After stirring, you should gently pat the surface flat with a bunched paper towel. If using your hand, wear a rubber glove or wash your hands well afterward. A bioactivated setup may not need substrate replacement for many years and will remain odorless and functional as long as you keep the substrate moist but never soggy.

You can place a layer of egg-crate plastic covered with plastic screening on the bottom of the cage before adding substrate.

Mixing in a drainage component such as seedling orchid bark, coarse sand, fired clays, or fired diatomaceous earth pellets helps aerate the soil and prevents it from compacting.

The trick to bioactivating a substrate is to weekly spray the inside of the tank and soil surface and stir the surface of the soil layer down to half its depth with a utensil such as a large plastic serving fork.

After stirring the soil, you should gently pat the surface flat with a bunched paper towel.

Plants

One of the many great features of crested geckos is that they make outstanding displays in planted naturalistic vivaria. Unlike many other nocturnal geckos, they will commonly rest on plants or between their leaves during the day.

Some of the new lines of artificial plants are very close in appearance to live plants and offer benefits for those who can't afford lights on their setups. Artificial plants don't need to be watered, they don't die, and they are not readily damaged. Another advantage from a design standpoint is that they don't grow. Your initial landscape composition will remain the same. The main flaw of artificial plants is simply that they are not alive. Only live plants can generate the feel of a simulated section of nature.

Functional live plants for crested geckos are species that fulfill essential niche requirements of crested geckos by providing activity areas, shelters, and basking sites. Functional live plants are a requirement for crested geckos unless one opts for artificial means of providing shelters and activity areas. When selecting plants, you should check that the leaves have sufficient rigidity to hold the weight of geckos.

Ornamental plants consist of species whose primary value is decorative rather than practical. As a rule, avoid plants with thin leaves because these will eventually be bent or torn as a result of a gecko's activities. Just one or two ornamental plants are all that is necessary to add an attractive decorative element to a vivarium. Remember that about half of a crested gecko's vivarium should be open space.

Plants can be introduced in vivaria either in pots or planted directly in a substrate layer. When planted directly in the vivarium substrate, plants contribute to the soil ecology, but their roots and growth can become invasive.

Artificial plants are easy to maintain.

Dracaena deremensis "Janet Craig compacta," a readily available cultivar, is enjoyed by crested geckos as a source of shelter.

Ficus benjamina ranks as one of the best functional species as long you use older plants with woody stems and thick foliage. This usually requires pruning to induce branching. The rooted cuttings with sparse foliage commonly offered in the plant trade are not as readily used by these lizards.

The plants shown here are types that primarily serve as shelters because of their stacked leaves. In general, species that have broad stacked leaves, such as some of the bromeliads (left), dracaenas (middle), and sansevierias (right), are good choices.

Vining or creeping plants such as the common pothos work well when allowed to crawl on a frame or down. Crested geckos use these as climbing areas and shelters. Smaller species of philodendron will also work well, e.g., the new cultivar Philodendron "Brazil."

Just one or two ornamental plants add an attractive decorative element to a vivarium. Remember that about half of a crested gecko's vivarium should be open space. Readily available species include orchids (left), anthuriums (middle), and aeschynanthus (right).

Many houseplants are raised under intensive pesticide treatment, and some soils may contain systemic pesticide granules. These are potentially harmful to your geckos. Before planting, it is generally a good idea to replace soil and wash leaves with a mild dishwashing detergent solution.

Keeping plants in pots allows for easy removal and to varying degrees limits growth.

Crested geckos are shrub- and tree-dwellers that like a combination of planted and open space. A good rule is to have about 50 percent open space interspersed with tall plants and dried wood sections.

Crested geckos generally appreciate some type of shelter, although this is not always necessary in planted tanks. As a rule, only use lightweight shelters to prevent any risk of accidental crushing.

Heating and Lighting

Anyone who has been lucky enough to visit New Caledonia knows that its climate is pretty close to paradise, seldom too hot or too cold, with the average daytime temperature around 78°F (25.5°C) and the relative humidity around 70 percent. Many keepers make the mistake of treating *Rhacodactylus* species as warm tropical animals, with the result that their geckos are often overheated and stressed. There have already been a number of reports of owners killing these geckos because they kept them too warm. Use a thermometer to assess the temperature under basking lights and in the shaded areas of the tank. Adjust the bulb wattage to establish the right temperature gradient. It should range from the low- to mid-70s° F (22–24°C) in the shade and up to 84°F (29°C) at the level of the top branches or other basking sites closest to the bulb(s). At night, lights should be turned off and the temperatures allowed to drop as low as 68°F (20°C) during spring through fall. During the winter months, night and day temperatures can safely drop by 10°F, down to the low 70s F during the day and low 60s F (17°C) at night.

Because crested geckos are active at night, they do not require supplemental lighting to fare well as long as they receive some indirect light from a lighted or windowed room. Hobbyists have successfully maintained and bred many generations of crested geckos with no additional light other than ceiling fluorescents and windows. However, providing a low-wattage incandescent bulb will allow you to grow live plants and to observe more natural behaviors such as resting in foliage under a heat source. In my experience, providing low-wattage heat lights can result in faster growth when raising *Rhacodactylus* species.

In typical setups, a 40-watt (for 20 gallons) to 60-watt (for more than 20 gallons) bulb in a reflector-type fixture resting on the screen top provides additional heat as well as light for growing plants. If possible, one of the bulbs should be a reptile UVB bulb, which can provide cresteds with ultraviolet–B radiation that hypothetically may help them synthesize vitamin D_3. I must emphasize that UVB-producing bulbs are absolutely not a requirement with crested geckos but simply an option. Most crested geckos are not raised under a UVB source and fare well with dietary D_3 in the form of vitamin/mineral supplements. Crested geckos will do fine with night temperatures in the 60s F (20°C), which is about the minimum at which most homes are maintained in the winter. Only if temperatures regularly dip below 55°F (13°C) would I consider providing a supplemental source of heat at night.

The easiest way to provide regular day/night light cycles is to plug their light units into an electrical timer. As a rule, the photoperiod should be 14 hours of light during the warm months, dropped to 10 hours during the cooler winter months. Heat can be controlled using either rheostats (these act as dimmers and must be adjusted manually to regulate the heat output, with the help of a thermometer) or on/off thermostats, which turn heaters on or off to achieve the set temperature. More sophisticated pulse proportional thermostats maintain a set temperature by essentially dimming the heat output to the desired level.

In naturalistic set-ups, low-wattage incandescent bulbs provide enough light for growing live plants and heat for crested geckos to bask.

To maintain a range of live plants, the best source of light is to have one or more fluorescent bulbs running the length of the enclosure (preferably one will be a UVB bulb). The number required depends on the width and height of the vivarium.

Low-wattage red incandescent bulbs are commonly used in areas where nighttime temperatures dip below 55ºF (13°C) in the home at night. Red bulbs also allow you to observe the activity of your lizards at night. Alternatives to red bulbs are the bluish types sold as moonlight bulbs.

The easiest way to provide regular day/night light cycles is to plug their light units into an electrical timer.

Mixing Species

Adults, not juveniles, of the smaller species of *Rhacodactylus* can usually be kept together with no problems. I commonly keep adult gargoyle geckos (*R. auriculatus*) with adult crested geckos. Others have kept *R. sarasinorum* and *R. chahoua* with cresteds. On the other hand, juvenile *Rhacodactylus* are best segregated by species. Young gargoyle geckos are notorious for tail-nipping and cannibalism when hungry and when size differences between members of a group become too great. This aggressive propensity abates with age, and they usually will not bother *Rhacodactylus* of similar size when adult.

Pink-tongued skinks (*Hemisphaeriodon gerrardii*) with an equal or larger SVL can be kept with crested geckos because of their specialized dietary habits. Their preferred foods are snails and slugs, but in captivity pink-tongued skinks will readily feed on certain types of moist cat foods (Whiskas mixed grill sold in pink pouches scored best in our tests). However, gravid female pink-tongued skinks should be removed from setups with adult cresteds and kept in a separate enclosure with a basking light. Pink-tongued skinks are live-bearers, and the tiny babies could become tasty morsels for hungry cresteds.

Adults of smaller Rhacodactylus species can be kept with pink-tongued skinks.

General Cage Maintenance

If using a simple setup, replace the paper substrate weekly. If using artificial grass carpet, clean it using a spray nozzle on a hose or in a tub with dish detergent. Clean the cage itself about every two weeks by taking it outdoors and spraying it down (for screen cages) or using a sponge and detergent (for plastic- or glass-sided enclosures). Cages can also be disinfected by soaking them in a 10 percent bleach solution. Always rinse artificial grass carpet and cages thoroughly after cleaning or disinfecting.

With naturalistic setups, the sides of the enclosure and plants should be sprayed once a week to allow fecal material and urates to fall to the substrate. When needed, use a sponge wet with just water to wash off the sides. With glass tanks, a plastic scrubbing pad or a razor blade is useful to remove caked fecal material. Do not use these with plastic-sided tanks or you will scratch them. After spraying down the tank, water is added as needed to moisten the substrate and water plants. Use any glass cleaner to clean the outside of glass tanks or sliding glass doors.

CHAPTER 6

FEEDING AND WATERING

C rested geckos are opportunistic insect and fruit eaters. In the wild, they may also feed on the nectar and pollen of certain flowers. In captivity, they thrive on commercially raised crickets, pureed diets (notably baby foods), and commercial crested gecko diet. Some adult individuals occasionally eat pink (newborn) mice.

Lightly supplement both crickets and pureed foods with a powdered vitamin-mineral reptile supplement and a calcium or calcium-vitamin D_3 supplement. Use calcium with D_3 if the vitamin-mineral supplement does not contain D_3. Crickets are dusted by placing them in a jar, adding a small amount of vitamin-mineral powder (a small pinch per adult or per 10 juveniles) and gently swirling the jar to coat them. Purees are supplemented by adding a similar amount of vitamin-mineral powder to the mix.

Specialist Allen Repashy, owner of the largest captive colony of *Rhacodactylus* geckos in the world, has formulated a complete diet for this species that is offered by T-Rex under the name Crested Gecko Diet. It is a complete diet that includes the calcium and vitamin D_3 necessary to prevent metabolic bone disease, as well as plant pigments to optimize the potential for bright colors. Combine one part of the powdered artificial diet with three parts water. To mix well, initially add a little bit of water and stir the mix until it becomes a paste. This paste will more readily blend with the rest of the water. The end result will be a liquid that quickly begins to thicken. The mix should be served soon after mixing to reduce settling. It can be left in the cage for up to 36 hours.

Crested geckos enjoy live insects; when possible, offer these once to twice a week. Providing live insects allows crested geckos to hunt and can help balance out their diet. Some breeders feed their crested geckos a diet primarily of insects with good results. Others feed them primarily supplemented pureed foods or artificial diets with equally good results. I personally offer mine T-Rex Crested Gecko Diet or pureed foods twice a week and insects once a week. Placing supplemented crickets in a bowl is one way to prevent them from scattering and can allow cresteds to free-feed whenever they are hungry.

The ideal diet provides some variety. For most of the year, crested geckos should be fed three times a week, preferably in the evening. During the cooler months of winter, crested geckos fare well with only one to two feedings a week. Some breeders will cool them down into the 60s°F (about 17°C) and not feed them at all for about a month.

The powdered Crested Gecko Diet is a complete diet that is easy to mix up for your crested geckos.

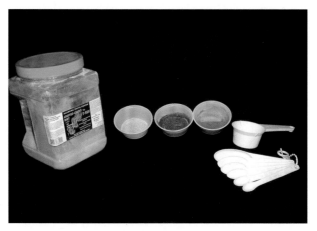

You can purchase the ingredients for an easy-to-mix diet at your local supermarket. Combine different baby food purees, usually 4 to 5 parts either banana, mixed fruit, apricot, or peach, with 1 part chicken.

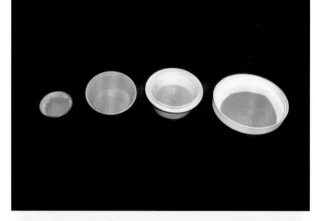

Offer your crested gecko pureed foods or Crested Gecko Diet in shallow food dishes. To estimate the amount, figure a volume about equal to that of the head of the gecko being fed.

Calcium carbonate or a calcium carbonate-D_3 powdered supplemented should be added to pureed foods. You can leave the food container in the enclosure for up to 36 hours. Many cresteds will decide to eat the food on the second day.

When possible, offer live insects to your crested geckos once to twice a week to allow crested geckos to hunt and help balance out their diet.

To gauge the right size cricket, figure that the length of the cricket should be no larger than the width of a gecko's head. Some breeders feed their crested geckos primarily supplemented crickets with very good success.

Most crested geckos do not readily feed on mealworms, but some adults will eventually learn to eat them.

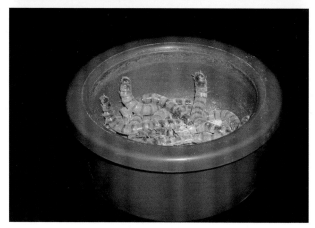

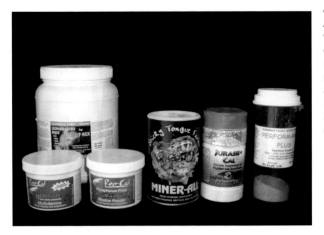

An easy way to prevent metabolic bone disease is to supplement the diet with a powdered calcium and a complete vitamin-mineral reptile supplement or with a calcium-D_3 powder.

Water and Humidity

Keep water available at all times in a shallow water container with a depth about equal to the thickness of a crested gecko's body. Replace the water and wash out the container with a detergent every two to three days. Thoroughly rinse after washing. Some keepers do not offer water dishes but simply mist the enclosure nightly, allowing their geckos to lick the droplets.

In the native habitat of crested geckos, the relative humidity is around 70 percent. In captivity they will tolerate a relative humidity of 50 to 90 percent. Relative humidity is measured with a hygrometer. Inexpensive hygrometers are now offered in the reptile trade.

To increase the relative humidity in dry climates, lightly mist the enclosure at least once a night. If you have a source of water in the enclosure—such as a water container, a moist substrate, or both—covering about half the screen top will also help raise relative humidity.

An ideal water container has a depth about equal to the thickness of a crested gecko's body.

Relative humidity is measured with a hygrometer.

Use a spray bottle to mist with water at night to increase the relative humidity of the enclosure.

CHAPTER 7

DISEASES AND DISORDERS

Signs of Disease in Crested Geckos

Generally, crested geckos are hardy lizards that are not prone to disease under the conditions usually provided in captivity. Realize that with crested geckos, as with most reptiles, disease is best prevented by providing optimal husbandry. Regularly monitoring and examining your geckos can help you detect signs of disease early on and allow successful treatment. The most commons signs of disease in crested geckos follow:

- *Weight loss*: Gradual or sudden weight loss is a consistent sign that a crested gecko is sick. Internal parasites are a common cause, but most other diseases eventually lead to weight loss because sick animals often don't feed. The first step is to get a fecal exam for parasites or bacterial infection and then follow the necessary course of treatment.

- *Lethargy*: Inactivity and sluggishness are common signs of disease, particularly when accompanied by other signs, such as weight loss.

- *Soft, bendable bones:* This is a sign of metabolic bone disease typically associated with calcium deficiency, insufficient vitamin D_3, or both. It often is noticed after the disease is advanced and when it's too late to easily treat animals. The first indication is usually soft jaw bones, noticeably of the thin lower jaw, making feeding difficult or impossible. In mild cases, deformities of the pelvis and floppy tail may also become apparent. Calcium-deficient females commonly become soft boned soon after eggs pass through the shell gland or soon after laying. Treatment is to administer calcium and vitamin D_3 orally, twice a day. If an animal is too weak or soft boned to swallow, you can administer calcium and D_3 directly into the stomach using a thin tuberculin syringe (no needle) or a thin feeding tube. In extreme cases, injectable calcium can be administered but will usually result in a gecko dropping its tail.

- *Twitching and muscle tremors:* This is usually the result of calcium deficiency and requires urgent treatment by administering calcium and vitamin C.
- *Shedding problems:* The failure to adequately shed, and perform skin removal and consumption is either due to low relative humidity or because a gecko is too sick to complete the shedding process. Maintaining adequate humidity levels of at least 50 percent usually prevents shedding problems. In dry areas, mist tanks nightly to increase the relative humidity. A common problem with geckos kept too dry is for shed skin to gather around toes, constricting them, cutting blood flow, and resulting in toe loss. If disease is the cause of shedding problems you will notice other signs associated with metabolic bone disease, such as lethargy or soft bones.

With regard to preventing disease, the best course of action is to provide optimal care, monitor animals daily, and consult with a qualified reptile veterinarian as soon as you notice the onset of the above signs. With smaller cresteds in particular, waiting until the symptoms are pronounced often results in the death of sick animals.

The most important procedure for preventing disease in captive reptiles is to quarantine newly obtained animals in basic setups located in a room distanced from one's established collection. To date, crested geckos have been relatively disease-free, but exposure to the pathogens of other species could change this before too long. Because many commercial breeders of crested geckos also work with other species, the spread of infections is a significant risk unless breeders implement and practice impeccable hygiene and disease prevention measures. As buyers, all we can do is to select animals and quarantine any new purchases for 30 to 60 days.

Tail Loss and Pelvic Deformities

Many lizards drop their tail in defense if they feel threatened. Unlike most geckos, crested geckos do not regenerate lost tails. In the wild, the great majority of adult crested geckos are tailless, and this may be considered the normal condition of adults of this species. If tails are lost at an early age, crested geckos typically regenerate a tiny, pointed tail stub. In captivity, the causes of lost tails are competitive fighting when young animals are kept in groups and fighting between adult males when more than two are kept together with females in the same enclosure.

Traumas, such as receiving an injection, overheating, or being startled by an unexpected grasping hand, also can lead to tail loss. Do not let the lack of a tail prevent you from buying a particular crested gecko. In the wild, adult cresteds are normally tailless and look more like little lizard-apes than little lizard-monkeys.

Pelvic deformities are common in crested geckos, even in the wild. The pelvic girdle of crested geckos, notably the ilial bones, consists of a thin framework. It is easily bent as a result of metabolic bone disease or simply stress from pressure exerted by the weight of a tail. Crested geckos that spend a great deal of time upside down on the vertical walls of a cage commonly have their tails bend to the side or over their back, with the result that the weight will bend the pelvic bones and eventually develop the syndrome called floppy tail. Commonly associated with floppy tail is a bending of the pelvic bones and possibly fracture of the zygapophyses (vertebral articular processes) at the base of the tail. There is no treatment for floppy tail. Unless the bend is so pronounced that the gecko appears deformed, floppy tail should not deter you from buying a specimen.

Dietary deficiencies can also cause floppy tail. A slight calcium deficiency may weaken thin bones, such as the pelvic ilial bones. Possibly, there is a genetic factor. Many crested geckos naturally develop a middorsal pelvic depression that may contribute to the syndrome. Worth noting is that in the wild, adult cresteds lack tails and that some also have bent pelvises. The easiest way to administer medication to crested geckos that are still eating is to mix it with baby food. This method can allow for easy treatment of large colonies.

If a crested is not readily feeding, you can use a syringe and apply drops of the medication on the snout, which usually induces a licking response. Once a gecko starts licking, you can gradually eject the medication until the necessary dose is administered. This method can also be used to administer a liquid diet to thin animals. Another method is to gently tap a gecko on the snout and, when it opens its mouth, eject the full dose of medication toward the back of the throat. Injecting medications is another option, but this procedure commonly leads to a crested gecko dropping its tail.

Quarantine new geckos for 30 to 60 days.

Crested geckos will sometimes experience shedding problems if ill or kept under conditions of low humidity.

Many lizards drop the tail if they feel threatened.

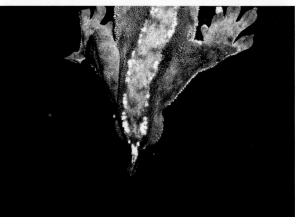

Trauma can also lead to tail loss.

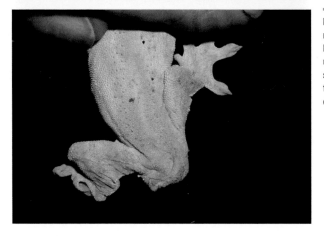

Floppy tail should not deter you from buying a specimen unless the bend is so pronounced that the gecko appears deformed.

Floppy tail is caused by the lizard resting for long periods of time on the sides of a tank so the tail flops to the side or over the head when a gecko is in a head-down position.

Many crested geckos naturally develop a middorsal pelvic depression that may contribute to the floppy tail syndrome.

A common mild sign of metabolic bone disease is a soft lower jaw. Even after treatment, a previously soft lower jaw may end up jutting out, resulting in an underbite.

Certain types of metabolic bone disease can result in irreversible deformities of the spine. In addition to calcium deficiency, oversupplementation with vitamin D3 is suspected to be associated with at least some cases of these spinal deformities.

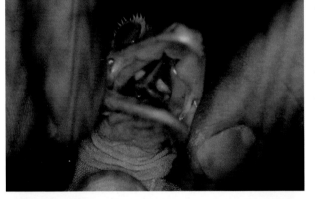

Crescent-shaped sacs at the back of the roof of the mouth store calcium. Calcium-deficient geckos' crescents are barely visible. Viewing these sacs with a bright light allows you to assess calcium reserves and predict the probability of a calcium crash.

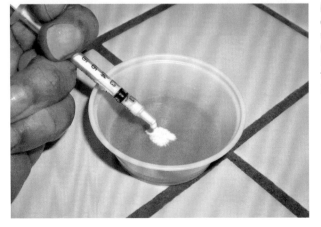

Here liquid fenbendazole (Panacur) is mixed with apricot baby food. This method can allow for easy treatment of large colonies.

CHAPTER 8

BREEDING

Crested geckos rank on a par with leopard geckos as some the easiest to breed of all lizards. Place an adult male and female together during the warm season and they will usually breed within a few months. For breeding purposes, crested geckos can be kept in single pairs or in harems consisting of one male with up to five females all year. As a rule, adult males should not be kept together in breeding groups because they tend to fight in the presence of females. The males may injure each other and end up losing their tails. Most breeders wait until females are at least 30 grams (an ounce) before putting them with males.

Crested geckos will breed readily during the warmer months of the year, usually from April through October. You should slightly cool their cages down from November to March, with night temperatures dropping into the 60°s F (about 17 to 20°C), which will usually stop breeding and egg production. A female produces about seven clutches of two eggs annually, with an interval of three to four weeks between clutches. Check the container daily during the breeding season if you are housing several females together. If you keep crested geckos in pairs, start checking about three weeks after the last clutch was laid.

When kept at around 82°F (28°C) and under intensive feeding regimes and supplementation with calcium and D_3, a female can produce up to 10 clutches annually, but this can be harmful. There is a record of a female laying 11 clutches but subsequently dying. A common pattern for females maintained under intensive regimes is for them to eventually calcium crash and develop sudden metabolic disease soon after a clutch of eggs passes through the shell gland. The shelling of eggs is a process that can cause a rapid drop in blood calcium. One way to stop females from laying eggs is to simply remove the male. She may lay another clutch or two but will eventually stop. This same method can be used to delay breeding in young females. If kept singly, they may lay a clutch or two of sterile eggs but will eventually stop laying them.

The male grasps the sides of the female's head or neck and positions himself for copulation.

Given the opportunity, crested geckos choose to lay their eggs in a moist substrate. In captivity, the preferred method is to introduce an egg-laying box–a container of moist peat moss–into the enclosure.

Female crested geckos burrow in moist substrate to lay eggs. Interestingly, they usually drop sterile eggs on the ground and don't bury them.

Transfer eggs within 24 hours of laying to an incubation container with 1.25-2 inches (3.2 to 5 cm) of a moist substrate.

As incubating media for crested geckos, coarse vermiculite (left), pure perlite (middle), and a 50-50 mix of vermiculite and perlite by volume (right) work well. Both vermiculite and perlite can be purchased at gardening supply stores.

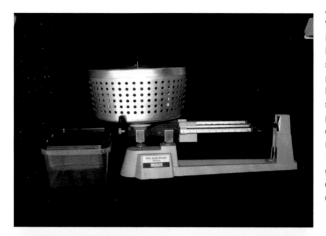

Weigh moisture of the incubating substrate. Five to 8 parts water should be added to 10 parts of dry substrate by weight (water should equal 50—80 percent of the weight of the incubating medium, e.g., add 1.75 ounces (50 grams) of water to 3.5 ounces (100 grams), of perlite.

Many hobbyists do not weigh the incubating medium, but simply gradually add water until it feels just moist and never so wet that water trickles between fingers when a handful is squeezed.

Before placing eggs in the box, label them to indicate parentage using a fine-tipped permanent marker. Half-bury them in the substance with labeled side up. Rotating an egg from its original positon usually ends up killing the embryo.

Incubating Crested Gecko Eggs

Only if your conditions are unusually cool should you resort to an incubator. An inexpensive incubator such as a Hova-Bator, carefully calibrated with the help of a thermometer, generally performs well when incubating these lizards. Place such incubators in locations slightly cooler than the desired temperature because they are capable of only heating, not cooling. Crested gecko eggs can be successfully incubated between 68°F and 84°F (20°C and 29°C) with an ideal temperature between 76°F and 78°F (24.5°C and 25.5°C). The eggs will survive night drops into the 60s°F (17-20°C), but avoid exposure to high temperatures (88°F [31°C] and above) as may occur during heat waves, which may be fatal. Depending on temperatures, the incubation time can range from 60 days (fluctuating temperatures of 78-84°F [25.5-29°C]) to 140 days (fluctuating temperatures of 68-72°F [20-22°C]).

Temperature-Dependent Sex Determination (TSD)

In many gecko species, sex is determined by the incubation temperature during the first two to three weeks of incubation. Setting the temperature at 76–78°F (24.5–25.5°C) will yield close to a 50-50 male to female ratio. If you want to skew the sex ratio, incubate eggs for the first three weeks at lower temperatures (68–72°F [20–22°C]) for a greater percentage of females, or at higher temperatures (80-85°F [26.5–29.5°C]) to obtain more males. After three weeks, reset the incubator to 76–78°F. More research is needed to clarify more precise parameters for TSD in this species. For more detailed information on TSD, the reader should refer to the valuable chapter on the subject by Brian Viets, PhD, in *The Leopard Gecko Manual.*

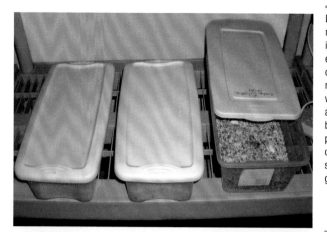

During the warm months of the year, incubating containers can be kept at comfortably warm room temperatures without resorting to an incubator. Most breeders simply place egg containers on a shelf in the same room as their geckos.

Only if your conditions are unusually cool should you resort to an incubator.

CHAPTER 9

OTHER RHACODACTYLUS SPECIES

For hobbyists seeking to expand their collections beyond crested geckos, the genus *Rhacodactylus* offers five additional species that differ significantly in appearance but that generally have similar requirements. They range from the medium-sized, knobby-headed gargoyle geckos to giants like *Rhacodactylus leachianus*, the largest of the living geckos. With the exception of giant live-bearing geckos (*R. trachyrhynchus*) all *Rhacodactylus* are now regularly captive-produced in large numbers and readily available.

Gargoyle geckos (*R. auriculatus*) are the second most popular of the *Rhacodactylus* species. They grow heavier than crested geckos and can be kept under similar conditions. Young gargoyle geckos are more competitive and prone to cannibalism than are crested geckos. Hungry babies will readily nip off the tails or toes of smaller specimens and, when size differences allow, even eat smaller cage mates. For this reason gargoyle geckos are best raised singly until they reach sexual onset.

Gargoyle geckos come in many patterns and colors. The most strikingly beautiful specimens diplay patterns with neon red or orange blotches or stripes. This species holds great promise for future development of new morphs. Their moderate size, low level of aggression, and unique appearance and hardiness make them one of the very best of all reptile pets. Like crested geckos, they make nice displays in naturalistic setups.

Looking for a large gecko? The largest of the living geckos is the Grande Terre giant gecko (*R. leachianus leachianus*) of New Caledonia. Type C (one of several morphs) reaches an SVL of 13 inches (33 cm), a total length of up to 17 inches (43 cm), and can weigh up to a pound (0.45 kilo). The most readily obtainable of the Grande Terre giant geckos are Type A. These reach an SVL up to 10 inches (25 cm), a total length of about 15 inches (38 cm), and can weigh up to 400 grams 14 ounces (.40 kilo).

A consistent difference between Grande Terre giant geckos (Type A) and the smaller Henkel's giant geckos (*R. leachianus henkeli*) is that the former have larger and more uniform snout scales. Grande Terre giant geckos also tend to have longer tails. They require three to five years to reach sexual maturity. Only a small number of these giants are in captive collections.

On the Isle of Pines and surrounding offshore islands live several morphs of Henkel's giant gecko. These don't get quite as large as Grande Terre giant geckos, up to about 12 inches (30 cm) total length, but they generally tend to be more patterned and attractive. At least six different population morphs of Henkel's giant geckos are established in captivity. A rare morph comes from the tiny island of Nuu Ana. Although these geckos are the smallest of the *R. leachianus* complex found to date, they are the most beautiful. They tend to be heavy-bodied and have bold, high-contrast, crisp-edged white blotches speckled with black. Herpetoculturists are striving to develop attractive morphs of Henkel's giant geckos by interbreeding.

One of the most responsive of the New Caledonian geckos is *R. chahoua*. They are the third largest species of *Rhacodactylus* with an SVL of $5^3/4$ inches (14.6 cm) and a total length of about 10 inches (25 cm). Their calm demeanor, complex mossy patterns, and large golden eyes with outrageous reticulated golden irises have made them a favorite of gecko hobbyists. They are found on both Grande Terre, the main island of New Caledonia, and on the Isle of Pines. They come in a mix of patterns and colors ranging from chocolate browns and tans to greens, bright reds, and pastel oranges. Some forms of *R. chahoua* have bright white blotches on their shoulders, and work is being done to assess the genetics of this trait. Only a small percentage of juveniles that hatch with a white shoulder patch retain them into adulthood. This species can be kept like crested geckos, but it prefers cork bark and thick branches as activity areas and usually will not climb in foliage. In a vivarium, *R. chahoua* often spends time in the open during the day and is a delight to keep and observe. Many become very tame.

Some gecko species give birth to live young. The largest of these is the Grande Terre giant live-bearing gecko, *R. trachyrhynchus trachyrhynchus*, which is also the second largest member of the genus after *R. leachianus*. These tree-dwellers are difficult to find and collect, and few specimens are in captivity. Long generation time and a low reproductive rate make them one of the most expensive lizards in the reptile hobby, and justifiably so. They require three or more years to reach sexual maturity and give birth to only two relatively large young per year. They are extremely alert and can be very personable. The other subspecies of giant live-bearing gecko, *R. trachyrhynchus trachycephalus*, occurs on a small island near the Isle of Pines and is one of the rarest and most endangered lizards in the world.

Rhacodactylus sarasinorum is a rare gecko with a very small distribution on southern Grande Terre. It is initially the most flighty of the species but eventually calms down and can make a nice pet. In setups with plants and climbing areas, *R. sarasinorum* spends a fair amount of time in the open and is enjoyable to observe. At the time of writing, relatively few specimens are produced in captivity, but this situation is bound to change as increasing numbers of hobbyists are recognizing the nice qualities of this gecko.

As with all *Rhacodactylus* species, *R. sarasinorum* displays some variation in color and pattern. One rare morph has a white collar and varying amounts of white blotches on the body. This is another promising species for selective breeding of new and colorful morphs. *R. sarasinorum* is the most slender-bodied of the *Rhacodactylus* species.

This is an example of a mottled morph gargoyle gecko.

A striped morph of the gargoyle gecko.

This is a Type A Grande Terre giant gecko, the most readily available type.

A consistent difference between Grande Terre giant geckos (Type A) and the smaller Henkel's giant geckos is the larger and more uniform snout scales, as shown in this close-up of a Grande Terre gecko.

Henkel's giant gecko is an attractively patterned gecko.

This is the rare morph of Henkel's giant gecko from the tiny island of Nuu Ana.

This is a female Nuu Ana x Nuu Ami cross showing unusually light coloration combined with large white blotches. She's grown larger than both her parents.

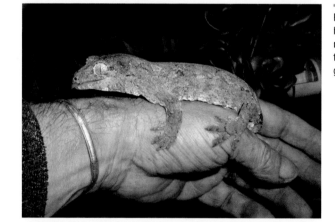

Rhacodactylus chahoua is one of the most responsive of the New Caledonian geckos.

Some forms of R. chahoua have a large, bright white blotch on their shoulders, as can be seen on this adult male. This species can be kept like crested geckos but prefers cork bark and thick branches as activity areas.

The Grande Terre giant live-bearing gecko, R. trachy-rhynchus, is difficult to find and collect.

Rhacodactylus sara-sinorum eventually calms down to make a nice pet.

This is a rare orange brindle morph of R. sarasinorum.

CONCLUSION

THE FUTURE

The future of crested geckos has been in part altered since their rediscovery. In their native habitat, notably on the Isle of Pines, crested geckos face several potential threats directly or indirectly related to man, such as the introduction of the nonnative little fire ant (a species with a nasty bite that can swarm and kill geckos) and the reduction or degradation of primary forest areas. As a result, at least some of the subpopulations may become threatened. On the bright side, the establishment of crested geckos in captivity has created a large alternate, self-sustaining population integrated in the human environment. This is in part due to the successful work of private herpetoculturists and their development of strikingly beautiful morphs with broad appeal. We can expect many more "flavors" of crested geckos in the coming years, a factor that will lead to even greater numbers and further increase their popularity.

The ready availability of crested geckos has also allowed for some experimentation in the design of innovative display systems that could prove valuable educational tools for teaching aspects of biology and ecology. Well-designed naturalistic setups simulate many important elements of ecology, including climatic factors such as light, temperature, and humidity, and biological factors such as plants, bioactive substrates, and various animals. Successfully keeping crested geckos with other species, such as pink-tongued skinks, allows one to study and understand some of the aspects of niche. Observations can also be made on the behaviors of animals and some aspects of their biology, such as growth rate, food conversion efficiency, and various aspects of reproduction. The great phenotypic variation in crested geckos offers opportunities for teaching and studying genetics. Multiple generations of crested geckos produced in a classroom setting can be recorded with a digital camera and can provide valuable data for understanding the underlying genetics of this polychromatic species. As long we make concerted efforts to maintain and advocate high standards of husbandry and humane care, the future of crested geckos in human society seems full of promise.

WORKS CITED AND RECOMMENDED READING

Bauer, A. M. and R. A. Sadlier. 2000. *The Herpetofauna of New Caledonia*. Saint Louis, MO: Society for the Study of Amphibians and Reptiles.

De Vosjoli, P., R. Klingenberg, R. Tremper, and B. Viets. 2004. *The Leopard Gecko Manual*. Irvine, CA: Advanced Vivarium Systems.

De Vosjoli, P., F. Fast, and Allen Repashy. 2003. *Rhacodactylus: The Complete Guide to Their Selection and Care*. Vista, CA: Advanced Visions (sales@giantgeckos.com).

Seipp. R. and F. W. Henkel. 2000. *Rhacodactylus: Biology, Natural History and Husbandry*. Lanesboro MN: Serpent's Tale.

INDEX

A
administering medications, 70
adults, 7, 29
aggression, 18–19
availability, 5–6

B
behavior: competitive fighting, 69; flight reactions, 15; group aggression, 18–19; jumping, 11; lethargic, 67; observing, 13; social, 15; threat displays, 13
bioactivated substrate, 48–49
breeding: breeding season, 74; commercial, 44, 48; enclosures for, 43–44; incubating eggs, 76–79; laying, 75; of *Rhacodactylus* species, 80–86; temperatures, 74
brindle morph, 29

C
calcium, 61, 63, 67–68, 73, 74
care/maintenance, 60
carpet chameleons *(Fur. lateralis)*, 19
characteristics, 7–13, 14, 22. *See also* colors; morphs
cloacal spur, 22
colors, 6, 25, 29. *See also* morphs
crests, 6, 7

D
dalmation morph, 29–30
defects, 38

deformities, 69–70
diet, 61–64, 69
diseases/disorders: administering medications, 70; metabolic bone disease (MBD), 61, 67–68, 74; parasites, 17; prevention, 68–69; signs of, 14, 67–68; tail loss/pelvic deformities, 69–70

E
embryonic stage, 18
enclosures: basic setups, 47–48; heating/lighting, 56–58; mixing species, 59, 87; naturalistic vivaria, 87; plants, 51–55; for quarantines, 17; selecting appropriate, 43–47
eyes, 12, 13, 14

F
Fast, Frank, 5
feeding, 61–64
females, 15, 19, 22, 24, 68
fighting, 69
fire morph, 29
flap-necked chameleons *(Chamealeo dilepsis)*, 18
flight reactions, 15
floppy tail, 48, 69, 71, 72
future of crested geckos, 87–88

G
gargoyle geckos *(R. auriculatus)*, 59, 80, 83
Grande Terre giant gecko *(R. leachianus leachianus)*, 81, 83, 84
Grande Terre giant live-bearing gecko *(R. trachyrhynchus trachyrhynchus)*, 82, 86

ABOUT THE AUTHOR

Philippe de Vosjoli is a highly acclaimed author of the best-selling reptile-care books, The Herpetocultural Library Series. His work in the field of herpetoculture has been recognized nationally and internationally for establishing high standards for amphibian and reptile care. His books, articles, and other writings have been praised and recommended by numerous herpetological societies, veterinarians, and other experts in the field. Philippe de Vosjoli was also the cofounder and president of The American Federation of Herpetoculturists, and was given the Josef Laszlo Memorial Award in 1995 for excellence in herpetoculture and his contribution to the advancement of the field.

REPTILES®

REPTILES magazine, the world's leading magazine devoted to reptiles and amphibians, has been entertaining, encouraging and educating fans of lizards, snakes, turtles and frogs for more than 15 years. An invaluable resource for any reptile lover, **REPTILES** magazine is the ultimate guide for owners and others interested in these fascinating exotic animals.

The World's Leading Reptile and Amphibian Magazine

Reptiles magazine will answer your herp questions:

· How can I keep my herps healthy?
· What is the best environment for my herps?
· How can I provide a balanced diet?

Plus

· Get the facts on nutrition and health care
· Save your issues for future reference on breeding and species profiles

Subscribe Today!
Reptilesmagazine.com/Anoles
or Call 1 (800) 876-9112

Outside the U.S. and Canada please call (515) 247-2981
Please allow 6-8 weeks for delivery.

E907YM1